Super Secret CODE BOOK

Fran Pickering

Illustrated by

John Pickering

Sterling Publishing Co., Inc. New York

If you haven't guessed it already, the cover code says:
A SIMPLE CODE FOR YOU TO CRACK

Library of Congress Cataloging-in-Publication Data Available

Pickering, Fran.
    Super-secret code book / by Fran Pickering ; illustrated by John
Pickering.
        p.   cm.
    Includes index.
    ISBN 0-8069-0890-4
    1. Cryptography—Juvenile literature.   I. Pickering, John (John
R. B.)   II. Title.
    Z103.3.P53   1995
    652'.8—dc20   94-23478
                                                      CIP
                                                       AC

1   3   5   7   9   10   8   6   4   2

Published by Sterling Publishing Company, Inc.
387 Park Avenue South, New York, N.Y. 10016
© 1995 by Fran Pickering
Distributed in Canada by Sterling Publishing
% Canadian Manda Group, One Atlantic Avenue, Suite 105
Toronto, Ontario, Canada M6K 3E7
Distributed in Great Britain and Europe by Cassell PLC
Villiers House, 41/47 Strand, London WC2N 5JE, England
Distributed in Australia by Capricorn Link (Australia) Pty Ltd.
P.O. Box 6651, Baulkham Hills, Business Centre,
NSW 2153, Australia
Printed and bound in Hong Kong
All rights reserved

Sterling ISBN 0-8069-0890-4

Contents

BEFORE YOU START CRACKING CODES, HERE IS A QUICK GUIDE AS TO THE LEVEL OF DIFFICULTY. WHEN YOU SEE ONE OF THESE SYMBOLS YOU'LL KNOW HOW HARD THE CODE IS LIKELY TO BE !

EASY
FOR A BRIGHT KID.

HARD
YOU'LL NEED TO THINK ABOUT THESE,

MEGA-HARD
YOU NEED TO BE A GENIUS!

Read and work through the first 22 pages to start with. They give basic information on codes and ciphers. If you get stuck, look back at these pages, especially at the hints on page 22 and at the clues on page 60.

Answers start on page 61.

WHAT IS A CODE?

A CODE is a word, group of letters or symbol that stands for another *word* or *group of words*. The coded word always has the same meaning. Shorthand is a code.

Have you ever written "&" instead of "and"? Every time you did that you were using a coded symbol. Other coded symbols you may have used are "+" for "add these together," "%" for "percent," and "°" for "degree."

SHORTHAND IS A CODE!

DEAR MR,...ER, NO... DEAR SIR,... I, ER... NO,...WE, WOULD, ER, HMM, ER,...

Below is a simple code. Can you guess what words the symbols stand for?

HAM & EGGS
BACON & TOMATO

You can find examples of symbol codes all around your house. Your iron may have spots or stars that indicate certain temperatures. Clothes may have symbols that mean they have to be dry-cleaned or can be tumble-dried. Furniture may have a symbol that means it is fireproof. Have a look!

6

One code that was more common in the 1920s and 1930s than nowadays is the American Hobo code. During the Depression years many people lost their homes and jobs and wandered the countryside looking for work. They often had to beg for food and a place to sleep at night. They would leave coded messages for each other so that those who followed would know if a certain house or farm or town was a good or bad place to call.

HERE ARE SOME OF THEIR CODED SIGNS. CAN YOU GUESS WHAT THEY MEAN?

HOW TO MAKE YOUR OWN CODE BOOK

YOU WILL NEED:
A SMALL NOTE BOOK,
A RULER AND
A PEN!

If you want to use a code book to send secret messages, you will also need to make a copy of the book for a friend.

1 DIVIDE EACH PAGE INTO 2 COLUMNS.

2

In the first half of the book, write down in the left-hand columns, in alphabetical order, all the words you might need to put into code. (You need to make a rough list first.)

If you find it hard to get started, put down the names of your friends, your family, street and house names, the name of your town, places you meet, and so on.

Then you'll need to add words and phrases such as, "go to," "meet me," "bring," "call," etc.

ANN	
Chris	
David	
FrANK	
Grove St.,	
HOMe	
JIM	
DAD	
NEW St.,	
ShoP	
School	

3

ANN	SEP
Chris	NEP
David	GROB
FrANK	DILLY
Grove St.,	ZAG
HOMe	CRIB
JIM	YARD
DAD	HEN
NEW St.,	ZIG
ShoP	REM
School	BUBBLE

Once you have your list, you need to give each item a code word, or group of letters. The code words can be real words with no connection to the items, or groups of letters chosen at random or to a plan. Make them easy to pronounce. Write these in the right-hand column.

In the second half of the book reverse this process. Write down all the code words in alphabetical order in the left-hand column and then in the right-hand column write the items that the code words stand for. Now you are ready to send and receive messages.

Another code that you may have heard about is MORSE CODE. In this code, patterns of dots represent letters, so Morse Code is really a CIPHER.

A .—	H	O ———	V ...—
B —...	I ..	P .——.	W .——
C —.—.	J .———	Q ——.—	X —..—
D —..	K —.—	R .—.	Y —.——
E .	L .—..	S ...	Z ——..
F ..—.	M ——	T —	
G ——.	N —.	U ..—	

WHAT ARE THE STARSHIP AND SPACE STATION SIGNALLING TO EACH OTHER?

SLL·SSSS·S·SLS·S·LSSS
LLL·SLL·S·SLSS·S·SL·SSSL
S·L·SSSS·S·SSS·SLLS
SL·LSLS·S·SSS·SSSS
SS·SLLS

SL·L·SL·SLLS
SL·SLS·LSL·SS·LS
LLS·LL·S·L·S·LLL·SLS

WHAT IS A **CIPHER?**

A **CIPHER** is a system in which each letter of the alphabet is replaced by a letter, number or symbol. Once you know the system, you can figure it out.

HERE IS THE WORD **CIPHER** WRITTEN IN MORSE CODE.

— • — • | • • | • — — — • | • • • • | • | • — • —

HERE IS A SIMPLE CIPHER!

A	B	C	D	E	F	G	H	I	J	K	L	M	N	O	P	Q	R	S	T	U	V	W	X	Y	Z
1	2	3	4	5	6	7	8	9	10	11	12	13	14	15	16	17	18	19	20	21	22	23	24	25	26

In this cipher, each letter of the alphabet is represented by a number. The numbers have been used in order from 1 to 26, but they could have been numbered like this:

A	B	C	D	E	F	G	H	I	J	K	L	M	N	O	P	Q	R	S	T	U	V	W	X	Y	Z
1	3	5	7	9	11	13	15	17	19	21	23	25	2	4	6	8	10	12	14	16	18	20	22	24	26

Here, first odd numbers are used and then even numbers. Instead of numbers we could have used letters of the alphabet, but arranged in a different way:

A	B	C	D	E	F	G	H	I	J	K	L	M	N	O	P	Q	R	S	T	U	V	W	X	Y	Z
N	O	P	Q	R	S	T	U	V	W	X	Y	Z	A	B	C	D	E	F	G	H	I	J	K	L	M

Here, the alphabet is split into two groups of 13 letters. The second group of 13 is placed in order under the first half of the alphabet, and vice versa.

TAKING THE EXAMPLES IN ORDER, TRY WRITING OUT THE WORD "CIPHER."

10

IF YOU ARE TRYING TO DECIPHER A CIPHER, HERE ARE SOME TIPS!

First of all, you need to narrow down what TYPE of cipher you are dealing with. Is it a TRANSPOSITION cipher—one in which someone has taken a message and rearranged the letters? Or is it a SUBSTITUTION CIPHER—one in which someone has substituted other letters, numbers or signs for the original letters?

If the cipher is made up of letters and you're not sure about it, do this:

Take a sheet of paper and write the alphabet in a column down the left-hand side.

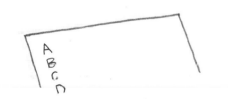

If the cipher contains numbers, signs, symbols, or pictures you KNOW it is a SUBSTITUTION cipher.

Here are the letters that are used most often in words in the English language: E-T-A-O-I-N (in that order. For example, most for E, etc).

If you have more checks for these letters, then the letters in the message have just been muddled up. If the checks you have don't match that pattern, then other letters have been substituted for the real ones.

Now read through the message and put a check next to every letter of the alphabet each time it appears in the message.

Here are the letters most often used in words in five other languages:

5 most frequently used letters:

German	E-N-I-R-S
French	E-A-I-S-T
Spanish	E-A-O-S-N
Portuguese	A-E-O-R-S
Italian	E-A-I-O-N

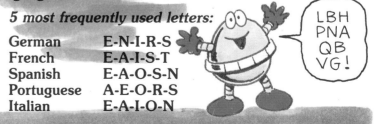

LBH PNA QB VG!

Letters of the English alphabet in the order they are most used in words:
E-T-A-O-I-N-S-H-R-D-L-U-C-M-P-F-Y-W-G-B-V-K-J-X-Z-Q

Can you work out the messages
in these codes?

1

14, 15, 23,
25, 15, 21,' 18, 5
7, 5, 20, 20, 9, 14, 7,
20, 8, 5   8, 1, 14, 7
15, 6, 9, 20!

2

13, 4, 4, 7. 13, 4, 17, 2, 13!
24, 4, 16. 1, 10, 9
12, 9, 5, 10, 9, 14
1, 13, 9, 2, 14
25, 1, 14, 9, 10, 17, 1, 23.

JRYY
QBAR
YRG'F
ZBIR BA
GB FBZR
ZBER

HOW TO MAKE YOUR OWN SECRET CIPHER SLIDE

YOU WILL NEED:

A sheet of thick paper or cardboard

A pen or pencil

One strip of paper or thin cardboard that is twice as wide as the sheet of cardboard and about half an inch (1.25cm) wide.

Small scissors

WHAT TO DO:

1. First write the alphabet clearly along the top of the sheet of thick paper, leaving a half inch (1.25cm) margin on each side.

2. Next, write the alphabet along the strip of thin cardboard, using the same spacing. You should get it on twice.

3. Cut two slits about half an inch (1.25cm) long in the sheet of paper, starting below the alphabet and about one-fifth-of-an-inch (.5 cm) in from the edge.

THIS IS KNOWN AS A; ST. CYR'S CIPHER SLIDE!

4. Slide the alphabet strip into the slots.

You now have your own cipher slide. Move the slide backward and forward to make different arrangements of letters that can be substituted for the alphabet. If your friends have a cipher slide as well, you can send each other coded messages and see who deciphers them first.

You can make your own version of the cipher slide by muddling up the order in which you write the alphabet letters on the strip, or by putting numbers in instead of letters. As long as your friends have exactly the same cipher on their strip, they will be able to work out the message.

St. Cyr's was the name of the French Military Academy where this cipher was taught in the 1880s.

Julius Caesar invented a simple cipher system that shifts the alphabet three places to the right.

HERE IS A VARIATION OF THE CAESAR CIPHER

Use a key word, no less than five letters long and with no repeating letters, to make a shift in the alphabet.

A B C D E F G H I J K L M N O P Q R S T U V W X Y Z
T E A C H I N G B D F J K L M O P Q R S U V W X Y Z

LIKE THIS!

AND NOW FOR THE
DATE SHIFT CIPHER!

Use a date—any date—to determine the symbol for each letter. For example, 11/5/22.

Write out the message: THE TRAIN WILL LEAVE AT ONE
Write the key number under it: 115 22115 2211 52211 52 211

The number under each letter tells us how many places FORWARD to shift that letter to get the enciphered letter.

For example: T+1 = U. H+1 = I. E+5 = J. T+2 = V.

so the coded message reads: UIJ VTBJS YKMM QGCWF FV QOF.

So, a letter in PLAIN TEXT (the original message) will not have the same number each time it is used.

Using the date 12/1/95, decipher this message:

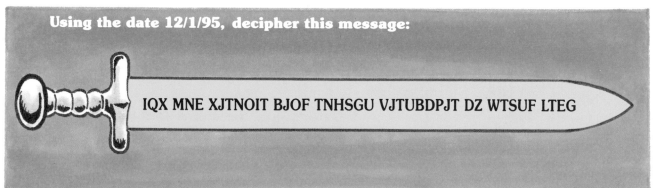

IQX MNE XJTNOIT BJOF TNHSGU VJTUBDPJT DZ WTSUF LTEG

THE DICTIONARY CIPHER!

You and your partner need to use the same dictionary for this cipher. Give each word a five-digit number. The first digits should be the page the word appears on. The next digits indicate the place on the page. If those work out to less than 5 digits, add zeros to bring it up to 5.

For example: Suppose "*hide*" was on page 696, and it was the 17th word on the page. Its code number would be:
69617

If "*address*" was on page 16, and it was the 15th word on the page, you would add 0 to bring the code number up to five digits and it would be: 16150

If you and your partner use copies of the same dictionary, you can easily look up a coded message.

To make things harder for someone trying to break your code, you could use even numbers for words in a left-hand column and odd numbers for words in a right-hand column.

LINE CIPHER

Take a piece of plain paper and write the alphabet across the top of it so that each letter lines up with a box on a piece of graph paper.

Now line up the graph paper and mark on it the position of the letters in the message you wish to send, in the order they appear in the message: the first letter on the top line of graph paper, the second letter on the second line, and so on.

For example: "SEND HELP" would look like this:

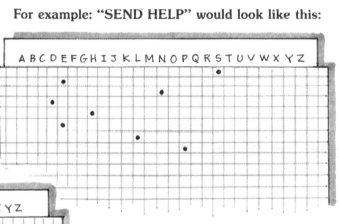

With the dots joined, it would look this this:

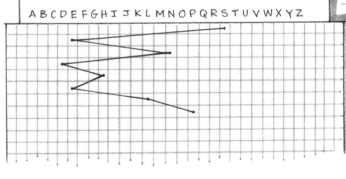

The paper on which you send the message has no alphabet on it, but the receivers of the message already have a sheet of paper with the alphabet correctly spaced out at the top. They line up the message underneath to read it. Try it!

Padrak lived in a country where people were not allowed to write and speak freely. He had published a newspaper that the State did not like, and the police had come to arrest him. As they came in the door, he pushed a piece of paper towards his secretary and whispered:

16

Sometimes there is no need to put a message into code. You can confuse people by the way you write it.

This is easy to read:

POPCORN IS GOOD FOR YOU. EAT A LOT!

This is not so easy:

PO PCO RNI SGO ODFO RYO UEA TAL OT!

TRY READING THIS!

1

SI XSW IF TSW IS SSHIP SSW IFT LYS HI FT

2 AND THIS

3

For this one you will have to make your own pattern out of the already muddled letters before you can read it. Here's a clue: 5 × 11

JONRY UUGEO SATSU TROOT IERNH NSEEI CTLTN AAAOK SRXGI ETHEN YIETG

HER	OKE	ION	ITT	HTH
ETH	NUP	SWH	ENI	ENR
EME	INT	ICH	NCO	EAD
SSA	OEV	ARE	LUM	UPA
GEI	ENS	THE	NSW	NDD
SBR	ECT	NWR	HIC	OWN

HERE'S A TIP!

How are the letters grouped? Look for a pattern. Try counting the number of letters in the message and then re-arranging them in different patterns. For example, if the message has 28 letters, you could make a block of 4 across and 7 down—or of 7 across and 4 down. Do the easiest and most obvious first, using as a clue the way the muddled letters are grouped. Are they in 4s or 7s?

One week a postman delivered a series of odd postcards to the house of a well-known research scientist. At the end of the week he went to the police. Why?

WONTD
ICOHG
LUNEE

TO:
DR. HUNTER
65 KINGSFIELD RD,
HAMILTON

LMSCB
HEAOR
ANTVI

TO:
DR. HUNTER
65 KINGSFIELD RD,
HAMILTON

NTUEN
DSRRG
OADEM

TO:
DR. HUNTER
65 KINGSFIELD RD,
HAMILTON

VTADO
ENYBN
ROBRE
DOYIY

TO:
DR. HUNTER
65 KINGSFIELD RD,
HAMILTON

19

Wizard Wonk decided to put his spell book into code in case someone tried to steal it. Now he doesn't know *what* this spell is for! Can you help?

HFW TF MFKF
F WFSH CFMF TRFF

TFKF F FLFKF FF FRFST
FN THF MFFNGLFW,
FND F DRFP FF DFW FN
THF DFWN.
MFX THFM BFTH WFTH
F CFP FF PFRF SNFW,
FND DRFNK FT FN FLL
HFLLFWS MFRN.

JUST IN CASE YOU GET STUCK, HERE ARE SOME
HELPFUL HINTS!

1. Have paper and pens handy. You'd be a true genius if you could solve these codes in your head!

2. DON'T PANIC! There are only so many variations on a theme and most of the codes in this book are *substitution codes*. That is: Letters, numbers, symbols or colors replace the letters of the alphabet.

3. Try the obvious first. Write out the alphabet. Then try fitting underneath it the letters, numbers or symbols in the code, in different combinations, until they make sense. The way the coded symbols fit will follow some familiar sequence. For instance; if colors are used, they may follow the order of the colors of the rainbow. Numbers may run consecutively, or all odd numbers first, or all even numbers, or they may be consecutive but in reversed order, and so on.

4. The examples of types of codes and ciphers have been put in the book for a reason. Maybe one of the codes to be cracked is a "Caesar Cipher," or a "Greek Square."

5. One or two codes have been put in just for fun (pages 28, 44–46, for example), and for you to guess at. You are not expected to know these, or be able to crack them, but the symbols themselves can be guessed at and you may turn out to be a good guesser!

6. Sometimes a message will not be encoded but just re-arranged into a less familiar pattern. Aim to unconfuse your mind by re-arranging the pattern or grouping of letters or by reading them in a different way, say up and down, rather than across.

7. Sometimes a well-known code will be used—but in disguise. Look for familiar patterns that will give you a clue. For example: On page 9 the Starship and Space Station are signalling to each other using a pattern of long and short radio waves. (You will have worked out that "S" stands for "Short" and "L" for "Long"). What well-known code is based on patterns of long and short groupings? Another well-known code that can be represented in a variety of ways is Semaphore. Study the semaphore code below and then try cracking the code on page 23.

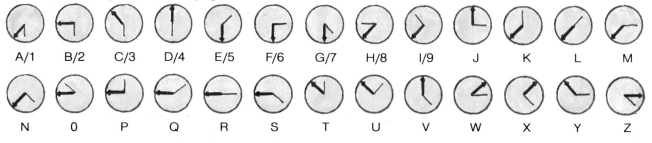

KIDNAPPED!

Millionaire Moneybags' daughter has been kidnapped. No one knows where she is and the ransom has to be paid by midnight or she dies. A boy on a bike, cycling in the countryside, is passing a deserted church. Suddenly, he notices the hands of the clock are moving. He watches for a while, then leaps on his bike and pedals furiously back to town.

**This is what he saw.
What did it mean?** →

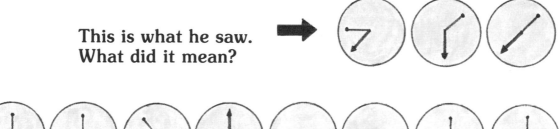

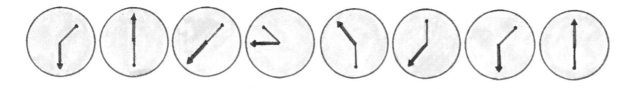

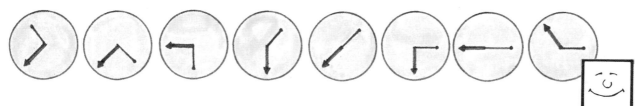

THOMAS JEFFERSON (1743–1826) once designed a substitution cipher. It was made of a set of 36 wooden discs roughly 1½ inches (3.8cm) in diameter and ¼ inch (.6cm) thick. Each disc had an alphabet in random order around the edge. The 36 discs were stacked together and held with a metal rod through the center. The discs were lined up so that the message appeared on one line across. The coder could then use ANY OTHER LINE for the enciphered message.

HOW TO MAKE YOUR OWN
JEFFERSON CIPHER WHEEL

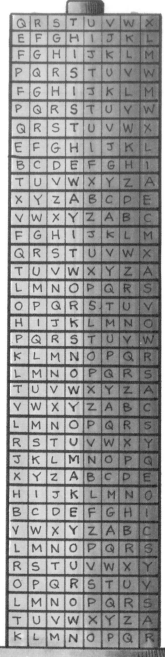

YOU WILL NEED:

A cardboard tube from inside a roll of kitchen towels
Sheet of paper 8½ inches (22 cm) wide by 7½ inches (19cm) deep
A pencil or pen   A ruler
Transparent tape   Scissors

1. Make marks at half inch (1cm) intervals across the top of the sheet. Draw vertical lines at these points to make **22 columns.**

2. Measure and mark 26⅓-inch (0.75cm) intervals down the right-hand side of the paper. Now draw 26 horizontal lines.

3. In the left-hand column write the alphabet, one letter per square. Repeat this in each column.

4. Cut along each column until you have 22 alphabet strips.

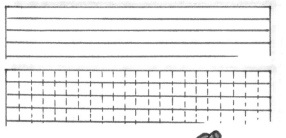

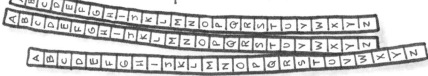

5. Wrap each strip around the tube and fasten with the tape. Make sure each strip moves easily and does not overlap another strip. If the strip is too long, don't overlap it but cut it so that both ends just meet.

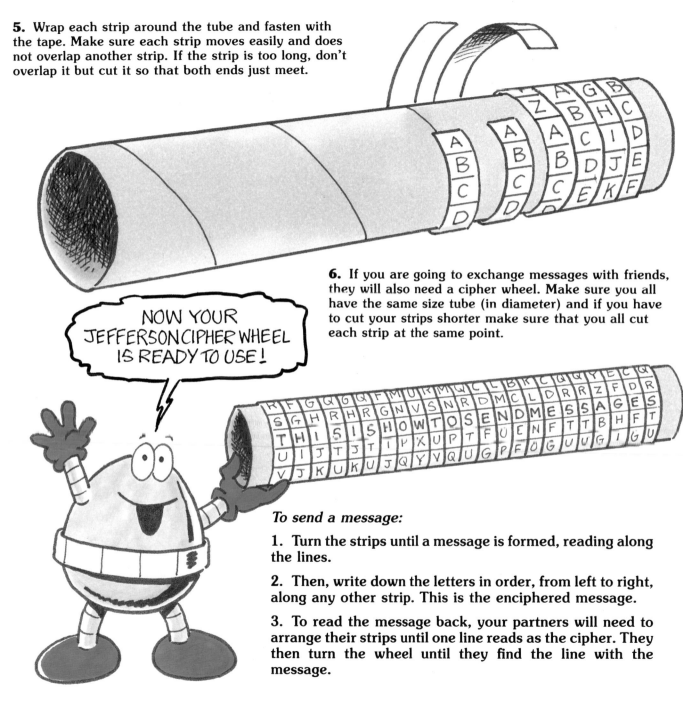

NOW YOUR JEFFERSON CIPHER WHEEL IS READY TO USE!

6. If you are going to exchange messages with friends, they will also need a cipher wheel. Make sure you all have the same size tube (in diameter) and if you have to cut your strips shorter make sure that you all cut each strip at the same point.

To send a message:

1. Turn the strips until a message is formed, reading along the lines.

2. Then, write down the letters in order, from left to right, along any other strip. This is the enciphered message.

3. To read the message back, your partners will need to arrange their strips until one line reads as the cipher. They then turn the wheel until they find the line with the message.

25

At the end of the 16th century, Mary, Queen of Scots, was imprisoned in the Tower of London by Elizabeth I. Mary sent secret messages in cipher to her friends. These were hidden in the hollow cork of a beer keg and sneaked out of the Tower by Gilbert Gifford, who was really a secret agent for Queen Elizabeth. Mary was convicted of treason on the evidence of her secret messages and beheaded.

Here is Mary's substitution cipher:

b g ω m H ꜀ f a ꜱ P k ꜱ ꙮ x ∞ : R b + ⊥ ⊥ ꝣ o⼐

a b c d e f g h i j k l m n o p q r s t u v w x y z

ε	e	∧	#	ꜱbʀо
and	as	by	for	mary

During the American Civil War secret messages were passed using a cipher known as the "Pigpen Cipher." You may need to use this elsewhere in the book!

A	B	C		J	K	L		S	T	U
• D	E	F	: M	N	O	: V	W	X
G	H	I		P	Q	R		Y	Z

The shape of a frame and the number of dots within it in a coded message tells you which grid it belongs to and so which letter it is. For instance:

⊡ = N   ⊔ = U

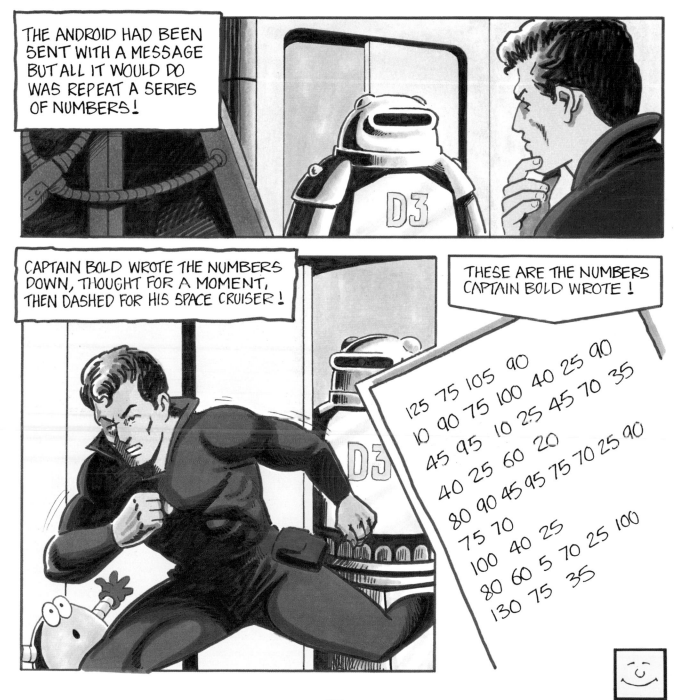

There was a young goblin, not very bright,
Who took up a pen and started to write.
What he wanted to say was clear in his head
But the words wouldn't come. He drew pictures instead.

NOT ALL CODES ARE WRITTEN. SOME ARE SPOKEN. HERE ARE A FEW YOU CAN TRY OUT WITH YOUR FRIENDS!

FIRST:
PIG LATIN

If you can learn to say this fast you can really baffle folks who don't know it. It works like this:

If the word begins with a VOWEL, add "WAY" to the end of it.

If the word begins with a CONSONANT, move the consonant to the end of the word and add "AY" after it. If the consonant sound is made up of 2 letters—move them both to the end.

HERE IS A SENTENCE TO PRACTICE IN PIG LATIN!

ISTHAY ODECAY ISWAY OTNAY EASYWAY OTAY AYSAY
UTBAY ONCEWAY OUYAY ETGAY ETHAY ANGHAY OFWAY ITWAY ITWAY
OUNDSSAY ERYVAY EFFECTIVEWAY.

This code is not easy to say, but once you get the hang of it, it sounds very effective.

OPISH

In this code you add "OP" after each CONSONANT. Try this sentence.

***TOPHOPE BOPIGOP BOPLOPACOPKOP BOPOOKOPSOPHOPOP =* THE BIG BLACK BOOKSHOP**

ABISH ENGLISH

This time you add "AB" before every VOWEL.

Here is the same sentence in Abish English:

***THABE BABIG BLABACK BABOABOKSHABOP =* THE BIG BLACK BOOKSHOP**

AGISH ENGLISH

SLURP!

Very similar to Abish English, but you add "AG" before each VOWEL.

Another sentence to try:

***BRAGOWN BAGEAGARS LAGIKE HAGONAGEY =* BROWN BEARS LIKE HONEY**

HONEY

Why not try making up your own spoken codes?

31

The earliest writing used in Egypt was made up of picture symbols. We call them *hieroglyphics.* Some signs represented a sound similar to one letter of our alphabet; some represented two or more sounds. Often a picture was drawn after a word to make its meaning clear.

Here are some hieroglyphics and the sounds nearest to them in our alphabet:

WHAT I SAID WAS: "TIME TO GO DOWN TO EGYPT!"...WHY NOT HAVE SOME FUN AND MAKE UP YOUR OWN FORM OF HIEROGLYPHICS!

M	F	P	B	W	I	A	Z OR S
S	CH OR SH	CH – AS IN SCOTTISH 'LOCH'	H	H	R	N	DJ
D	TH	T	G	K	Q	SH	

The Travellers had come to the end of their journey. Their way was barred by a door sealed years ago by a magic word. Only that word would open it. None of them knew what the word was, but they hoped a clue would be on the door itself. What was the word?

TEUSDD
HAGPTE
ERHEHN
PTTAET
UHTKWE
RAOFOR
EVFRRH
OEEIDE
FNAEAR
HARNNE

One type of substitution cipher, which is more than 2,000 years old, uses two symbols for each letter of the plain text (message). This is called a "Greek Square." The letters of the alphabet are put into a grid, the sides and top of which are numbered. I and J are put together. It would look like this:

	1	2	3	4	5
1	A	B	C	D	E
2	F	G	H	IJ	K
3	L	M	N	O	P
4	Q	R	S	T	U
5	V	W	X	Y	Z

So the name "BERYL" would be enciphered like this:

B=12, E=15, R=42, Y=54, L=31 = 1215425431.

In the examples below, Agent X has encoded two messages using two different variations of a Greek Square. Can you work them out?

1. **6265 63619265719581 9385746593 619265 65016592040273659265**

2. **BEAEAECE DECE DDBCAE BBCDCDAD EBCDDBBE**

Here the symbols have been separated into words to help you. If you wanted to make your message harder for an enemy to read, you would not do this.

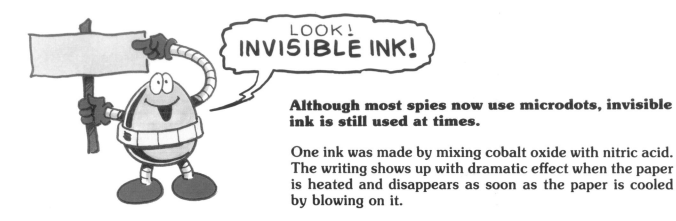

Although most spies now use microdots, invisible ink is still used at times.

One ink was made by mixing cobalt oxide with nitric acid. The writing shows up with dramatic effect when the paper is heated and disappears as soon as the paper is cooled by blowing on it.

During World War II the Germans used a special tablet that looked like an aspirin to turn ordinary ink into invisible ink. The writing was visible while the message was being written, but then it disappeared after it had been exposed to the air for a few minutes.

Also during World War II, hundreds of thousands of letters were read and censored in England, mainly at Liverpool. A team of 1,700 language experts were kept busy looking for coded words or messages written in invisible ink.

Spies sometimes have to eat their words when they need to destroy a code sheet or message in a hurry. Two types of *edible* paper are used: **Balsam,** which is a Japanese tissue-paper, and **Rice Paper,** which you may have eaten on the bottom of homemade meringues or macaroons.

Ovid (Ancient Roman poet), knew that milk could be used for secret writing on parchment. Gentle heat made the writing appear. He recommended it to secret lovers in one of his poems!

WHY NOT TRY MAKING YOUR OWN INVISIBLE INK? HERE ARE SOME WAYS TO DO THIS!

To write in invisible ink, use a pen with a steel nib, such as a fountain pen or calligraphy pen. Make sure that the nib is clean or the writing will not fade properly.

LEMON JUICE

Squeeze the juice of half a lemon into an egg-cup and use it to write your message. When the juice dries, your message will be invisible. Simply iron the paper at a low heat to reveal the message.

RICE WATER

If your mother is cooking rice, then ask her to pour a little of the rice water into a cup before it all boils away. When it is cool, write your message. To reveal it, dampen the paper and hold it over a bottle of iodine for a few minutes.

YOU WILL NEED THE HELP OF YOUR SCIENCE OR CHEMISTRY TEACHER TO MAKE THE FOLLOWING INVISIBLE INKS.

COBALT NITRATE

Dissolve one teaspoon of cobalt nitrate or cobalt chloride in a cup of water. You will then have a pink solution that will become invisible as you write with it. When held in front of a hairdryer or heater, the writing will show up as deep green.

COPPER SULPHATE

Dissolve one teaspoon of copper sulphate in a glass of water and use this to write your message. To read the message: Dissolve one teaspoonful of sodium carbonate in 4 fluid ounces (118ml) of water and pour this into a flat dish. Immerse the sheet of paper in the fluid, and the writing will turn blue. If you leave the paper to dry, the writing will turn brown.

REMEMBER, ASK YOUR TEACHER FOR HELP WITH THESE!

Walking in the woods, Walter found a strange box inside a hollow tree. (He always looked in hollow trees, hoping that something interesting would be hidden in them!) Inside the box was a tiny black seed. The underside of the lid had a pattern carved on it. Walter wondered if the pattern meant anything! Did it?

Duncan was writing a book. He hadn't gotten very far, because it kept coming out wrong. This is what he had written so far:

40

Cedric liked to write to his friends in code.

HERE ARE A FEW OLD TIPS FOR PASSING ON HIDDEN MESSAGES!

In England in the 1700s and 1800s it cost more to send a letter than a newspaper, so people used newspapers to send secret messages. They picked out the message one letter at a time by making a hole just above each printed letter with a pin. The person receiving the newspaper would look for the pinholes and spell out the message.

In the 12th century, Genghis Khan, whose empire stretched from China to the Black Sea, developed a mounted courier service called the "*yam*" to carry secret military and political messages.

Centuries ago the Chinese trained swallows to carry their secret messages. No one knows how they did this, since swallows are not as easy to train as pigeons.

I HOPE THIS IS THE RIGHT WAY!

GREECE

Histiaeus, Greek Ambassador to Persia, sent secret reports home by a very strange method. He found a slave with poor eyesight, shaved his head and had the message branded on his skull. When the slave's hair grew back, Histiaeus would send him off to Greece, telling him that his eyesight would be cured when his head was re-shaved on his arrival in Greece!

I JUST WISH HE'D LEARN TO WRITE IN SHORTHAND!

Tacitus, a Roman historian, told of secret messages being hidden inside bandages on wounded soldiers, or sewn into the sole of a shoe. A more clever method was to write the message on a thin sheet of lead, which was then rolled into an earring.

44

Wouldn't it be great to be able to talk in sign language? Below are the 26 basic signs from one of the hand-signal languages used by deaf people. This is a very useful language to know. Why not learn these signs and practice using them with your friends?

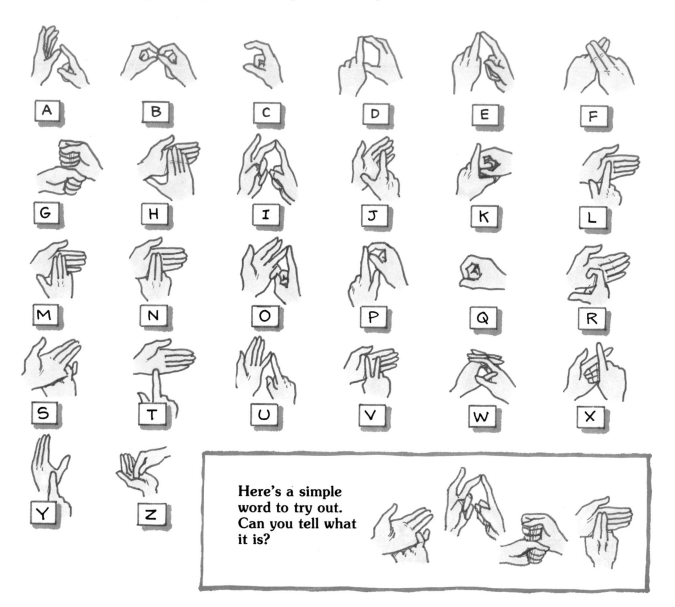

Here's a simple word to try out. Can you tell what it is?

Julie Crockett collected old things. She was also an ace private eye. This time, hot on the trail of a dangerous criminal, she had left in a hurry. On her desk was a note for her assistant, in code. Can you decipher it?

4/1.6/3.6/2.3/2.
2/1.3/3.8/1.3/2.7/2.
2/2.4/3.4/1. 4/2.2/1.7/2.7/2.9/3.
4/2.3/2.4/3.7/3.8/1.
7/1.5/3.2/1.6/2.6/2.3/2.3/1.
3/3.6/3.7/2.
6/1.4/3.3/1.6/2.4/3.4/1.4/2.8/1.
8/1.3/2.5/3.5/3.
3/1.3/2.8/1.3/2.2/3.8/1.4/3.8/3.3/2.
7/3.6/1.4/3.8/1.4/2.

Plans for the new spacecraft were top secret. Only one man knew where the complete blueprint was kept and he had disappeared. Then, one of the team found a metal box with four numbered buttons on it. Wired to it was an explosive device. If the wrong button was pressed, the whole thing would explode. In the pocket of a jacket hanging on the door, the team also found a paper with numbers on it, four of which were the same as those on the buttons. Could it show them which button to press?

I THINK THAT THIS COULD BE SOME KIND OF CODED MESSAGE!

$28 \div 2$	6×10	$40 + 28$	12×6	$36 \div 4$	$51 \div 3$	$66 - 10$	32×3
$70 \div 10$	18×3	13×3	1×6	$43 - 6$	$23 + 7$	$8 + 19$	$47 - 7$
$50 + 8$	$76 \div 4$	$22 - 2$	14×3	$75 \div 5$	$49 + 6$	38×2	$100 \div 4$
$31 + 7$	$45 + 3$	$68 \div 2$	$96 - 12$	37×2	25×2	$30 \div 6$	$63 + 7$
4×4	$56 \div 2$	7×7	$39 + 27$	11×2	$60 - 15$	$26 \div 2$	$54 + 40$
$15 + 3$	$80 \div 8$	$74 + 12$	$27 \div 9$	$46 \div 2$	$19 + 32$	$58 \div 2$	16×2
3×12	$93 \div 3$	$55 \div 5$	$94 \div 2$	$24 \div 7$	17×5	9×7	$42 + 4$
10×10	5×15	$29 - 3$	$48 \div 6$	$34 + 9$	$20 \div 5$	$86 + 7$	$72 + 8$

96   73   85   4

Rosco was visiting his friend Carrie. Carrie was crazy about puzzles and gadgets. Everything in her house was part of a puzzle. Even the front doorbell had a computer code that Carrie changed daily. Rosco looked at today's code and wondered which button to press. He read the letters one by one.

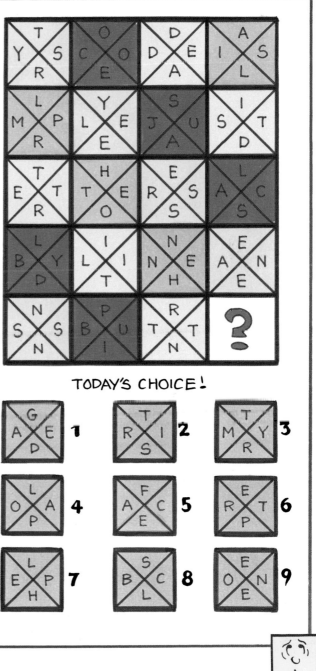

TODAY'S CHOICE!

50

This is a substitution cipher.

Swift-fingered Sam was up to his old tricks—robbing safes. This time it looked like he'd met his match. A computerized touch-pad opened the lock and each button had to be pressed in a certain order. An incorrect sequence would set off the alarm. Which button should Sam press first?

	1	2	3	4	5
A	3S	2E	1S	4S	2W
B	1S	2S	2E	3W	1S
C	1E	2N	2S	1S	2W
D	4E	1E	LAST	2N	3N
E	4N	3N	1W	1E	4W

CLUE:

Start at the end and work back!

Blyn was a bard of ancient time,
Who spoke a great deal but only in rhyme.
When he fell in love, he became a bit mushy.
And this verse that he wrote is a little bit
slushy.

What did he say?
Can you work it out?

My *first* is in *water* and also in *wet*;
My *second* in *tortoise*, a family pet.
My *third* and my *fourth* both show in my *will*,
Doubly in *ill* and the medicine *pill*.
My *fifth* you can see when I'm thinking of *you*,
My *sixth* you'll see twice if you think of me *too*.
My *seventh* is heaven when *under* your spell,
Under enchantment in *you* I dwell.
My *eighth* is in *marriage* and *merriment* gay,
My *ninth* in the *act* and also the *play*.
Ten and *eleven* in *two hearts* entwine;
Twelve mirrors the *fifth* if you sift through this rhyme.
Thirteen's unlucky for some, so they say,
But here brings a *promise* that I give today.
Last but not least, at the end of the *line*
Fourteen rounds off this proposal of *mine*.

SSHH! NOT MANY PEOPLE KNOW THIS!

During the Civil War a man named J.O. Kerbey would spend his days leaning idly beside the window of the telegraph office in Richmond, Virginia, which was the headquarters of the Confederate Army. He appeared to be enjoying the warmth of the sun and lazing his time away. In fact, he was a Federal spy who could read Morse Code at high speed and was listening to the telegraph operator tapping out messages. He memorized these and later wrote them down and sent them to federal headquarters in Washington. He managed to get away with this all through the war and ended up a second lieutenant in the Federal Army.

An ancient Greek method of sending secret messages was to write them on wooden tablets that were then covered with wax. A fake message was carved on the wax. The receiver of the tablet simply melted the wax to reveal the hidden message.

A king of Spain once complained that the French must be using black magic to break his codes. In World War II, the Americans code-named their cipher department "Magic."

In the early 1970s U.S. military intelligence was estimated to transmit more than 300,000 coded messages daily.

Writer Edgar Allan Poe used a cipher system in his story "The Gold Bug."

THAT'S THE HEAD OF OUR CIPHER DEPARTMENT!

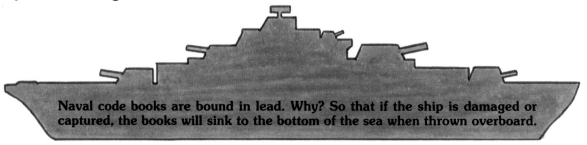

Naval code books are bound in lead. Why? So that if the ship is damaged or captured, the books will sink to the bottom of the sea when thrown overboard.

Pirate Pete's crew has found this document on the ship they have just raided. Pete thinks it is worth more than all the treasure they plundered. Why?

2S.3S.1S.1C. 1S.1C. 2S.3S.4S. 1S1C.4S.4S.1S1C. 1C.3S.
1C.4S.3S.4S.1S1C1S.1C.3S.1S.1S1C. 2S.1C. 2S.3S.4S. 1S.1C.2S.3S.3S.1S1C. 1C.3S.
4S.1S.1S1C1S. 1C.3S. 4S.3S.1S.1C.3S. 1S.1C. 3S.1S.1S1C.1S1C. 4S.3S. 3S.2S.2S.
4S.3S. 3S.3S.1S2C.1C.2S.1C.1C.1C. 4S.4S.3S.2S.2S.3S. 2S.1C. 2S.3S.4S.
1S2C.4S.3S.1S1C1S.4S.1S1C1S. 1C.3S. 2S.3S.1S.1C. 1S1C.4S.4S.1S1C. 4S.3S.
1C.4S.1S1C1S.2S.3S.3S.2S.1C. 4S.1S.2S.2S. 1C2S.1S.2S.4S. 2S.3S.4S.
2S.1C. 4S.3S. 1S1C.3S.2S.3S.1C.4S. 3S.3S.1C.4S.1S.3S.1C2S. 2S.3S.3S.2S. 3S.
3S.4S. 1S1C.4S.3S.1S1C. 3S.3S.1S1C. 3S.3S.2S.4S. 1C.3S.1C.1C.4S.3S. 4S.3S.
1C.1C.1C.1C.4S.1C.1C.1C.1S1C1S. 1C.1S.1C2S.3S.4S.1S1C.
1C.1C.2S.3S.4S.3S.3S.-2S.3S.4S.-4S.1S.1C2S.3S.2S.3S.

HERE'S A CLUE!

Look at the shapes of the letters of the alphabet. Are they curved or straight?

George was a computer expert and a top secret agent. He had hacked his way almost to the secret files he wanted. He needed one last password. Whatever he tried, the screen continued to display the same pattern of colors. What was the password he needed?

Entering Professor Hubert Zweistein's laboratory, the student found it empty. Glancing around, he noticed on the bench a puzzle that the famous nuclear scientist had been working on. Idly, the student began completing it, while he waited for the Professor to return. When he reached the end, he phoned the Research Institute's Security Department. Why?

AGATE	(AGENTS)	NIGHTS
ABOUND	( )	USUFRUCT
HUBBUB	( )	EFFORT
FUSS	( )	IMPRESSION
SEC	( )	RACKET
STEREO	( )	LEAVEN
AIM	( )	ICING
CAIRN	( )	AGENDA
FOAL	( )	LONG-BOW
REMISS	( )	CURLICUE

The Binary Twins were talking too fast for Maisie to understand, and her pocket translator had jammed after the first word. Can you help her work out what they are saying?

BOP:

11001.101.10011.   1.1110.100.

1001.10100.

10011.10000.101.1.1011.10011.   10011.1111.

10011.10100.10010.1.1110.1111.101.1100.11001.

BIP:

10111.1000.1.10100.   1.

10111.101.1001.10010.100

11.10010.101.1.10100.10101.10010.101.

CODE CRACKING CLUES

Page 7: Unless you know the hobo code, you'll have to guess on this one.

Page 9: S could mean "short" and L "long."

Page 12: Look back at page 10.

Page 14: Count 3 places FORWARD to encipher, 3 places BACK to decipher.

Page 16: Remember Caesar. What has he got to do with cupboards?

Page 17: Look back at page 9.

Page 18: 5 × 11.

Page 19: Look back at page 18.

Page 20: Maybe Big Troll should have used other letters instead of R?

Page 21: Remember Big Troll.

Page 23: Imagine the clock hands as arms holding flags.

Page 27: Read page 22.

Page 28: This is a rebus.

Page 29: Look at the longship.

Page 33: Look at the hieroglyphics on page 32 and guess at the rest!

Page 34: Look back at page 10.

Page 35: Try arranging different combinations of numbers or letters around the grid.

Page 38: Look at page 26.

Page 39: What is Duncan writing on? Is he confused?

Page 40: Substitution cipher.

Page 41: Remember Caesar, but do more than he did!

Page 43: Look back at page 10.

Page 44: No clue—just guess.

Page 47: Look at the telephone.

Page 48: The first thing to find is which square to start in. Try the obvious first. Start where all numbers start.

Page 49: Look back at page 18.

Page 51: Read each number individually, even if it's in a pair. For instance, one-four—not 14.

Page 52: Think of the compass points. One move to the south would be one move down.

Page 53: A good old-fashioned riddle.

Page 55: 2S.3S.4S. = THE
2S.1C. = TO
4S.3S. = MY

Page 56: Read page 22. Remember the rainbow.

Page 57: Look for the connection between the word in the brackets and the words on either side.

Page 58: If you can substitute numbers for letters of the alphabet, maybe you can substitute symbols for numbers?

Page 59: Think of computer language.

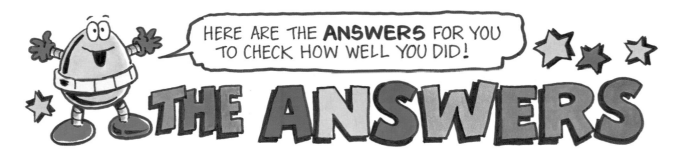

Page 6: Parking. Ladies Restoom. Restaurant. Airport.

Page 7: 1. very good. 2. gentleman. 3. if sick, will care for you. 4. doctor.

Page 9: Morse Code.
STARSHIP: *Where do we leave the spaceship?*
SPACE STATION: *At a parking meteor!*

Page 10: 3, 9, 16, 8, 5, 18
5, 17, 6, 15, 9, 10
PVCURE

Page 11: The Robot is saying "YOU CAN DO IT!" using the third cipher on Page 10.

Page 12: 1) *Now you're getting the hang of it!*
2) *Good going! You are secret agent material.*
3) *Well done! Let's move on to some more.)*

Page 14. *How Did Vikings Send Secret Messages? By Norse Code!*

Page 16: Keyword Cipher. Use "Cupboard" to shift the alphabet along. For example:
A B C D E F G H I J K L M N O P Q R S T U V W X Y Z
C U P B O A R D E F G H I J K L M N Q S T V W X Y Z
Message: *"My manuscript is under the loose floorboard. Send it to a publisher abroad."*

Page 17: "Eeek! A Hideous Little Bug!" (Morse Code)

Page 18: 1. "Six swift Swiss ships swiftly shift."
2. "Here the message is broken up into even sections and then written in columns that read up and down."

3. "*Just in case you are starting to relax, here's one to get you thinking!*" (To read this, you need to re-write the letters in a block 5 across × 11 deep.)

Page 19: When all the groups of letters were put together to make a block 5 wide × 13 deep, they bore a message that read: *"Will Hand Over Documents At Noon On Saturday By The Covered Bridge. Bring Money."*

Page 20: Big Troll had put an "R" in place of every vowel. Message reads: *"Dear Snotrot, Please come by on Thursday. Love from Grizzleguts"*

Page 21: Dizzy Wizard Wonk put "f's" in place of all the vowels in his spell. It should have read:

HOW TO MAKE A WISH COME TRUE

Take a flake of frost in the moonglow
And a drop of dew in the dawn.
Mix them both with a cup of pure snow
And drink it on All Hallow's morn.

Page 23: Message: *"Help! Kidnapped! Locked in belfry!"* She used the hands of the clock to form semaphore signals.

Page 27: Message: *"Your brother is being held prisoner on the planet Zog!"* Numerical substitution, starting at 5 for A and going up in 5's. So B=10, C=15, and so on.

Page 28: This is a rebus. In a rebus, pictures or symbols are substituted for words—or parts of words. Letter reads: *"Dear Guy. I'll meet you Sunday at Snake Rock to look for spiders and frogs. Love, Bill"*

Page 29: Message: *"Don't bother to come back. You took all we had last time. Signed: Your Mother."*

Page 33: Message: *"My Mummy has gone (g+one) shopping for dog food."*

Page 34: The word is "FRIEND." Reading down each column from the left the clue is:
"The pure of heart have naught to fear,
Speak 'friend,' the word, and enter here."

Page 35:

	1	2	3	4	5
6	A	B	C	D	E
7	F	G	H	IJ	K
8	L	M	N	O	P
9	Q	R	S	T	U
0	V	W	X	Y	Z

*Be careful
Spies are
everywhere*

	A	B	C	D	E
A	A	B	C	D	E
B	F	G	H	IJ	K
C	L	M	N	O	P
D	Q	R	S	T	U
E	V	W	X	Y	Z

*Keep up
the good work*

Page 38: Pigpen Cipher (see Page 26). Message: *"This is the seed of the Tree of Dreams."*

Page 39: Duncan had gotten the letters on the keyboard muddled up with the letters of the alphabet! Substitution cipher:

Alphabet: A B C D E F G H I J K L M N O P Q R S T
Keyboard: Q W E R T Y U I O P A S D F G H J K L Z

U V W X Y Z
X C V B N M

Story: *"Once upon a time, in a land far away, there lived a dragon."*

Page 40: Message: *"The numbers are a substitution cipher for the alphabet. If you crack this code you can be excused from homework for one week!"*

A B C D E F G H I J K L M N O P Q R S T
26 25 24 23 22 21 20 19 18 17 16 15 14 1 2 3 4 5 6 7

U V W X Y Z
8 9 10 11 12 13

Page 41: Substitution cipher: Taking the pictures in order, write down the names of the objects under the letters of the alphabet. For example:

A B C D E F G H I J K L M N O P Q R S T U V W X Y Z
W O L F/ M O N K E Y/ P I G/ S N A K E / C O W/ Z E B R A

Message: *"Dear Melvyn, I made this code as hard as I could. I hope you enjoy it. I'm looking forward to our picnic next week. Shall I bring some popcorn? Love, Cedric."*

Page 43: Roman numerals substituted for alphabet:

A	B	C	D	E	F	G	H	I	J	K	L	M	N	O
I	II	III	IV	V	VI	VII	VIII	IX	X	XI	XII	XIII	XIV	XV

P	Q	R	S	T	U	V	W	X
XVI	XVII	XVIII	XIX	XX	XXI	XXII	XXIII	XXIV

Y	Z
XXV	XXVI

Message: *"Send two more legions and lots of food."*

Pages 44/45: 1. Go this way. 2. I went this way. 3. Trail goes this way. 4. A note is hidden 6 steps in this direction. 5. Short distance this way. 6. I went this way. 7. Go over water. 8. 3 miles this way. 9. Long distance this way. 10. Trail goes this way. 11. Not this way

Page 46: Sign.

Page 47: Julie used the dial of her old telephone to make a coded message. Each dial number also has 3 letters with it. Giving them each a position number of 1, 2 or 3, reading from left to right, Julie was able to substitute a number for each letter. For example: "L" would be 5/3—third letter along at number 5. Message: *"Gone after Big Harry. Heist planned for midnight. Tell Detective Smith."*

Page 48: Button 85. There is no clear indication with this type of code of where to start, so always try the obvious first. Remember that on page 22 we wrote that symbols would always follow a familiar sequence. So, if dealing with numbers, it is reasonable to look for Number 1 and start there. Starting at 1×6, the answer to each sum leads you to the next button. For example: $1 \times 6 = 6$. Go to the square with 6 as the top number—that is, 6 $\times$ 10 $\times$ 60. Next square is 60 $-$ 15, and so on.

Page 49: Button nine. Message: *"Today's code is really simple. Just read the letters across line by line and then press button nine."*

Pages 50/51: Message: *"We will be with you in half an hour. Put the coffee on!"* Starting at A, letters are numbered: 1(One), 1-1 (One-One), 1-2 (One-Two), and so on, to 1-10, then 2 (Two), 2-1 (Two-One), 2-2 (Two-Two), and so on. For example:

A	B	C	D	E	F	G	H	I	J	K	L	M	N	O	P	Q	R	S	T	U
1	11	12	13	14	15	16	17	18	19	110	2	21	22	23	24	25	26	27	28	29

V	W	X	Y	Z
210	3	31	32	33

Page 52: C4. Each button moves you on to another button. For example, 1S means move to the next button south (one down). To work out which button to start from, you need to work backwards from the button marked "LAST." Correct sequence is: C4, D4, B4, B1, C1, C2, A2, A4, E4, E5, E1, A1, D1, D5, A5, A3, B3, B5, C5, C3, E3, E2, B2, D2, LAST.

Page 53: Message: *"Will you marry me?"*
1=W (in *water* and *wet*); 2=1 (in *tortoise*); 3&4=LL (in *will*, *ill* and *pill*); 5=Y (in *you*); 6=O (in *too*); 7=U (in *under* and *you*); 8=M (in *marriage* and *merriment*) 9=A (in *act* and *play*); 10&1=R (in *hearts* and *hearts*); 12=Y; 13=M (in *promise*); 14=E (in *line* and *mine*)

Page 55: Substitution:
  S stands for the number of straight lines in a letter
  C stands for the number of curved lines in a letter

Once you know this, it is just a matter of trying different letters with the same combinations until you get a word that seems right. As you progress, the other words in the sentence and the overall sense should indicate whether a word is correct or not.

A	B	C	D	E	F	G	H	I	J	K	L	M	N	O	P
3S	1S2C	1C	1S1C	4S	3S	1C2S	3S	1S	2S1C	3S	2S	4S	3S	1C	1S1C

Q	R	S	T	U	V	W	X	Y	Z
1C1S	1S1C1S	1C	2S	1C	2S	4S	2S	3S	3S

Message: *"This is the deed of ownership to the island of Mir, on which is hidden all my fabulous wealth. To the*
bearer of this deed my servants will give the key to my palace, knowing that I am dead and have chosen my successor. Signed. Sulaman-The-Mighty."

Page 56. George!
The colors represent a substitution cipher, colors for letters. The colors are the colors of the rainbow in order: Red, orange, yellow, green, blue, indigo, violet: A = red; B = orange; C = yellow, and so on. Each color will represent three or four letters. You will need to work out which letter fits best. This will become easier as you progress. When translated the message reads: *"Top Secret. Authorized Personnel Only. State Name."*

Page 57: He ran to the telephone to summon help because the puzzle turned out to be a secret message that read: *"Agents abduct Hubert. Fusion Secret Stolen. Aiming Canada. Follow. Rescue."*

The word in each bracket is formed from the first *two* letters and the *last* letter of the word *before* the brackets, and the *first* letter and *last two* letters of the word *after* the brackets.

Page 58: Button number 20. Each shape has a numerical total: □ = 6; ○ = 2; △ = 4; □ = 8

Thus the row with the question mark adds up to 20.

Page 59: Substitution code. Letters of the alphabet are numbered from 1 to 26 in order, but using the binary system of numbering.

A	B	C	D	E	F	G	H	I	J	K
1	10	11	100	101	110	111	1000	1001	1010	1011

L	M	N	O	P	Q	R	S
1100	1101	1110	1111	10000	10001	10010	10011

T	U	V	W	X	Y	Z
10100	10101	10110	10111	11000	11001	11010

Message: BIP: What a weird creature.
BOP: Yes, and it speaks so strangely.

INDEX